REV. KEMI

WHISPER
OF THE FLAME

AN INNER JOURNEY INTO YOUR SACRED FLAME WITHIN

ISBN: 978-1-4525-5299-6 (sc)
ISBN: 978-1-4525-5298-9 (e)

Library of Congress Control Number: 2012909858

Balboa Press books may be ordered through booksellers or by contacting:

Balboa Press
A Division of Hay House
1663 Liberty Drive
Bloomington, IN 47403
www.balboapress.com
1-(877) 407-4847

Because of the dynamic nature of the Internet, any web addresses or links contained in this book may have changed since publication and may no longer be valid. The views expressed in this work are solely those of the author and do not necessarily reflect the views of the publisher, and the publisher hereby disclaims any responsibility for them.

"All the concentrated darkness in the world
Cannot even put down one single flame"/ Lady Ruth

Any people depicted in stock imagery provided by Thinkstock are models, and such images are being used for illustrative purposes only.
Certain stock imagery © Thinkstock.

Printed in the United States of America

Balboa Press rev. date: 11/28/2012

BALBOA.
PRESS
A DIVISION OF HAY HOUSE

"There is an infinite Flame, glowing endlessly in you.

Emanating from GOD'S eternal flame.

Connect to the source of your flame.

Be the 'Igniter' of flames in others.

Be the flame that shines and does not burn...

Wherever you go...", Rev. Kemi Nahal

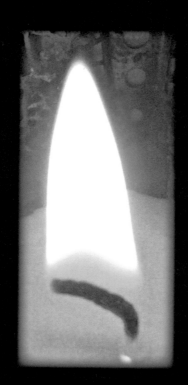

2

"When everything calms down and silence enters the walls of the world.. A dream comes true.." Rev. Kemi Nahal

"All the concentrated darkness in the world

Cannot even put down one single flame"/ Lady Ruth

Personal Message

"You are a flame

in God's living fire,

You are the dancing flame in God's Infinite furnace...

You are the Flame endlessly glowing

In God's heart"...

Feel the warmth of God's flame within your heart ...

The Flame Speaks to you, listen... as the light travels into space...,

Listen to the 'Whisper of the Flame'...

Carrying you on.."/ Rev. Kemi Nahal

Dedication

"To my Creator, The source and The Keeper of my Flame -

GOD the Almighty, forever glowing - living in me"/Kemi Nahal

Acknowledgement and Gratitude

To my dearest spiritual teacher – Leo, thank you for your living and loving light. For all the sacred esoteric knowledge & the high connections you have taught me, for your sincere care and devotion. For 'The WAY' and for all that you are. I cherish you always and forever, glowing 'in-me-ay'/Keeper of The Flame, Deer-Spirit

For all my precious guardian angels and all God's angels & archangels, masters and guides – To all the great ones who show me how.. Thank you all... Thank you for your light and love.

To my precious and dear Lord Jesus the Christ – the true Jesus Christ –Yehoshua – 'Prince of Ruby' –the living flame in my heart and soul. Thank you Jesus for your holy omnipresence and guidance, teachings, healing and help within my soul and throughout this Earthly journey and forever more.

For the Beloved Saint Germain, for the ancient life times you have taught me of the sacred teachings and connections to The Violet Flame and the I AM presence within. I cherished it through space and Time. I know it's Time, Now! Thank you for always being here and there...

To my Dearest true Gurus of GOD, Shiridi Sai Baba and Amma. Thank you for Your Love and Light.. for all the Miracles you perform in my Life.. and for your Sweet Loving teaching and pure Light..

To All The Light Beings and the White Brotherhood and the Order of the high priesthood of Melchizedek, Thank you for your guidance, teachings and help. Thank you for responding to my call at any time I was and am in need.

To the most amazing divine Healer of Light – John of God. Thank you for your long life devotion and sacrifice at service to GOD and Humanity. Thank you for the Healing Miracles, sincere Care and Love. I Love you very much. "I kiss the Hands of the Healer".

Thank you – My dear Flame, for your friendship and wisdom, for carrying my prayers and wishes. My dreams and conversations.. For your wisdom and your help, for lighting up my room, my home, each day, each night... For your faithfulness, each time I call upon you and light up a candle, you always come. Thank you endless Flame of GOD. Thank you for warming up my heart and soul.. I love you dear Flame of GOD, Forever shining in me, forever glowing in me.

Thank you God, for your Glorious Infinite Flame.

A special Thank You note for my dear children Oriya and Emmanuel for their love and sweet Light.. I love you dearly, May God's Light always shine upon you and in you wherever you'll be. And for my darling boyfriend Gerald, for your sincere care and true love, for supporting, helping and believing in my dreams. Thank you for everything.

To my dearest aunts & grandmas - Rebecca and Vicky, Kamila and Emma. And my holy grandpa Ezra Nehmad. Thank you for your prayers and love.

My Love to you ALL, Rev. Kemi Nahal (Deer-Spirit-Star)

"There is a part in me that I journey into,
As I walk on this marvelous Earth,
I walk into the sacred Earth within me.
The Heavens shine upon all Earths.
And the joy of being..
Emanates from
The flame in the midst of it all..." Kemi Nahal

A great master called me 'Glorious Flame', come, sit by my lamp, listen to the subtle flickering sound of the Flame. Watch its dance, come dance, feel the warmth of the Living Fire.

"Kindling a candle

It's for the kind and the pure of heart". Kemi Nahal

The soul rejoices to the light of the candle...

Come sit by the fire.

The silence of the Flame speaks of the great endeavors of the light.

Traveling, being moved by the great creator, caring marvelous intelligence.

Inspiring each time, each moment to ride, to carry on..

Come sit by the fire, warm your being.

The inner cool blue at the center of the flame resonates with
the stillness of your inner life, the core of your being.

The flame within you, slowly, making known to you now.

Its' appearance may come as the ocean waves, rising from within.

You emerge...

You connect to your inner core..

You remember the Sun within you, the three fold Flames within your heart.

And the hidden passages to the other realms.

Come sit by the fire.

Touch the softness of the flame, feel the joyful blazing dance
of life, expressed so beautifully by the Flame.

The love of the creator is in each flame, in each sparkle, in each dance.

Be at peace, know that all is well, no matter where you are, you carry the
flame of the most high within you. Connect to it, reach within, feel its warmth
and its endless power ceaselessly glowing, shining, dancing within you.

With each sunrise - rise with each sunset - pause for a moment,
wonder . . . of what the horizon brings your way .. Dwell for a
moment.. Imagine hope and peace in the hearts of all living.. Listen
to the inner dance of the flame that never cease to glow...

The Flame invites you to dance.

Dance...

The Flame speaks to you, listen

Touch your heart... It speaks to you.

Listen,

Feel the Flame within you, dancing with joy.

Dance, dance with joy.

You are alive!

Dance with joy.

I light a candle each day.

Once, as I stood lighting a candle an ancient being appeared

Softly spoke and said "Keeper of The Flame".

I am the Flame!

I am the Illuminating Flame and the Light

Rejoice.

I am with you each time you light a candle.

I am with you each time you light up someone's life.

I am with you when you felt alone and cold in the dark places.

Didn't you see the Light you shined? Try to remember, even there in the
dark you were shining, for GOD is within you no matter where you are.

Realize it, see it, feel it,

You are glowing wherever you are, even when you cry.

Don't let your heart be bothered, call upon me "Keeper of the Flame",
I am only a whisper away, never left you, I am always with you.

I ignite you, I empower you, I nourish your being with Light and
wisdom, each and every step of the way. I am with you,

Light beings encompass you then and now. They know and see your light from the core
of the universe. Your vibrations rising, you feel the warmth of your existence, come.

Listen to the Tales of the Flame where knights and wizards
set, where angels gathered, just like then, it is now.

Shh... shh.... The Flame is aglow. Listen...

Sit by your Flame.

Last night, I cried, something in me
felt alone, for long moments.

I asked where are you dear One?

Dear One.. Dear Way, Please don't leave me.

The tears I shed, reminded me
the warmth of The Flame.

As I write this down now,

I realize. He came. He was right here, then and now.

I fell asleep feeling its warmth in me, enveloping my being.

In the morning he came again.

I spoke the silence of the Flame.

Sometimes it is silent,

Yet it is always here and there.

God never leaves us.

Sit by the silence of the Flame. It will carry your thoughts.

It will speak wisdom to your Being. Your Soul will make
an appearance. You'll hear its heavenly voice.

HOLY.. HOLY is the Flame OF LIFE.

HOLY FLAME. speak to me.

In the silence there are words that cannot be said, only feelings. We watch, sense, we go within. We see from a different part in us, we are being.

In the silence, we listen.

We grasp,

We connect,

We can be approached,

The heavens are watching us all the time.

The Heavens speak,

Listen.

Until one day, in the stillness

We become The Flame.

The heaven's gate opens, in the middle of the sky...

It can be seen from where you are.

Make offerings to the fire...

There are divine beings standing by the fire,

Sitting, dancing in the Flames..

Make an offering to the Fire.

Feed it with goodness and quality of foods.

Ask for your prayers to be carried to the Heavens through the holy flames.

There are fairies and 'little people', essences, unseen living
things, which live by and in the flames.

Perhaps one day, you will see the unseen lives that are in the Flame.

Things of kind are gentle yet powerful.

For they know LOVE.

They are infinite.

They feel your vibrations

They see your light,

Wait by the Flame

They will come.

Staring at the candle light

I felt the warmth of its life,

*I knew I wasn't alone. Even a little candle light can warm
your heart in the midst of a storm, or late at night.*

Even a little candle light can fill up your entire being with light.

Share the light. Expend it, no matter where you are.

Become that light, that flame, that does not burn... always glowing,

Shining eternally illuminated from within...

A great prophet wrote words of Ruby Light, so bright.

I know! I believe he sat by the Flame
that knows all things.

23

Protect you 'Inner Flame'.

There are troubling things in this world, big storms and blowing winds...

Sometimes they pass by.

Don't be afraid. For nothing can put your flame down.

Within you is the Eternal Flame, created by GOD.

Remember the source of your flame.

Remember the very thing that ignited your flame when you were created . . .

Shining in you . . .

Shine on your everlasting light.

Grow your light, expand it like the universe. Keep expanding, growing,

Feel the flame within your heart.

Love

Feel... Love... Be full of LOVE...

You are the Love in the center of your flame

Your heart is 'flammable'...

Love ignites the heart.

Oh Love... The flames of love, dancing within my heart.

God's presence enveloping me, filling me with joyous spirit.

I smile to God. God smiles within my heart.

Do you feel it?

Love is flammable.

The heart loves to dance with joy,

Buoyant spirited flame of GOD, dance with me,

Dance in me.

The graceful dance of the Flame inspires one to sit and wonder by its light.

Dance little Flame, dance.

Joyful flame, dance...

The Living Flame... The Living Fire... The Living GOD, lives within you..

And if you are of kind, The living flame of GOD will envelop you. It will show you far places as you'll travel the light. It will carry you on. Perhaps you'll discover and remember once again, the Inner Temples of the Living Flame.

Resonating with the flame, opens wondrous doors, revealing higher dimensions, places you might have known before.

Holy, Holy is the Living Flame.

The Flame knows your heart.

I smile back to the Flame...

The Flame whispers and smiles back to me.

Smile more often. Laugh. Laugh more.

Cheer,

Love,

Be blissful,

The Flame knows its bliss.

The tree knows its bliss.

The ocean, the Bird, the flowers,

It is all Bliss...

LIFE IS BLISS

Bliss All Around

In Hebrew ꞉ LEHAVA means =FLAME

(Lehava) = להבה

Heart‑ in Hebrew pronounce ‑ Lev = לֵב

GOD=ה',ה

God's Heart –

It means and sounds in Hebrew – Lehava = a Flame

Flame of God = (Lehava) = להבה – Flame

Remember

Let me tell you a little story said the Flame

In an old village surrounded by a great forest lived an old man. He was a very kind and loving man. He was a very wise man.

People came to him seeking help and counsel. He mixed herbs for healing and laid hands on the sick. He gave presents and played with the children and told them stories of enchanted places and of ancient Time.

Story time became a time of evening gathering of the villagers where they shared baked goods and warm cider and tea. The old man's name was known to many and expended to far countries. They called him the man from the Stars and The White Wise old Man. He knew the stars.. He knew great the Secrets of the Universe.

One day, a young man came to the see the old man. He greeted the young man with a warm smile and let him in.

'What's your name young man?' asked the old man.

The young man hardly could sound his name and burst in tears. Carefully watching the young man crying, the man from the stars reached to a shelf in his herbal medicine cabinet and chose some herbs, and then he warmed water to make a tea for the young man. He held a small clear crystal shaped like a chalice and gently scooped a blend of herbs and mixed it. The water was ready to make a special tea.

'Dear young man, I can see your pain' Said the man from the stars. 'You'll be alright.. This situation, this phase in your life will change and improve for you'.

Then the wise old man from the stars held a white a silvery feather of a legendary bird and gently held it closer by the young man's face.. Tears dripped onto the white silvery feather.. While the young man was still weeping..

'Please drink some tea'. Said the old man from the stars.

Holding the legendary silvery feather above the crystal chalice, the old man from the stars let the tear drops drip into the crystal chalice. As the tears dripped into the crystal the young man slowed down. He paused for a moment and raised his head and looked at the old man. The old man reached to the young man's face and gathered more tears, held the legendary feather above the small crystal chalice.. And let the tears drip into it.. It filled up with the young man's tears...

The young man started to calm down, he took a deep short breath.. And made a sigh.. ahh..

The old man from the stars turned towards the young man.. his blue eyes were glowing bright light.. his face was shining and his entire being became aglow.

Mesmerized by the beautiful beaming sight, the young man felt his being uplifted, enhanced.. Then the old man laid hands above the Crystal Chalice and chanted ancient prayers. Suddenly the young man noticed a marvelous flame appeared inside the crystal chalice. His tears transformed into a beautiful shimmering light of blue, indigo and silver, outlined in gold, glowing and moving from side to side, inward and outward. The room was filled with splendor. As the young man kept looking at this very rare and beautiful sight, he forgot his sorrow, he felt he was now in a different place... everything around him changed... The Flame spoke, and the young man suddenly felt his Inner Flame Within his Heart.

As he took a deeper breath, he felt his inner flame growing bigger, emanating from within, and expanding from within and throughout his entire being.

The young man got in touch with his inner flame...

Feeling highly moved and enhanced by this experience, the young man realized he has reached and got in touch with his ultimate inner source of light, and his Inner Flame, he saw and felt the source of his flame. He felt oneness with the cause and the Giver of His Flame. He was silent for very long moments...

Not interrupting the young man's holy place, the old man from the stars quietly placed the crystal chalice in a velvet pouch and placed it on the table in front of the young man to take with him.

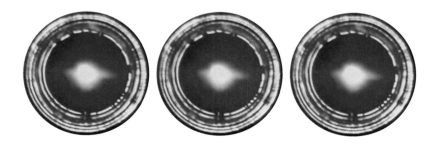

Awakened and aglow the young man opened his eyes and smiled to the old man. 'Thank you Grandfather Star, thank you said the young man.

'Now that you found it – keep it Alive in YOU! Keep in touch with it. You'll see wonders and miracles. You'll reach heights and places you never knew are there... places you forgot will become known again...' said Grandfather Star.

'It will make and keep you illuminated. That's what IT does. It will light wisdom in you to have understating and will shine the light of great knowledge.' You'll understand great mysteries and learn and know the way of the universe. The source of it all resides inside you'. 'It only can happen if a man's heart and being is clean and pure'. The old man added.

The young man sipped from the tea listening to Grandfather Star.

The night grew older. They sat and pondered the wondrous mysteries of the Universe. Watching the magical Flame in the middle of the room.

'The Inner Flame is

The Mover'...

Connect to the Mover of All Flames

Dance around the Flame..

Always be careful.. flames are 'flammable'...

Fairies are gathering around the flame. Dancing joyfully.
Round and around.. Giggling.. Loving the dance.. Loving the Flame...

*Watching the candle flame bring joy and comfort...

Loving is keeping the flame alive...

Loving is keeping the flame alive...

Flames of love are stronger than a camp fire..

Love

Keep loving,

Let the flame within you grow bigger and brighter..

Love..

Love warmth the heart..

Flames of love, are stronger than all hatred..

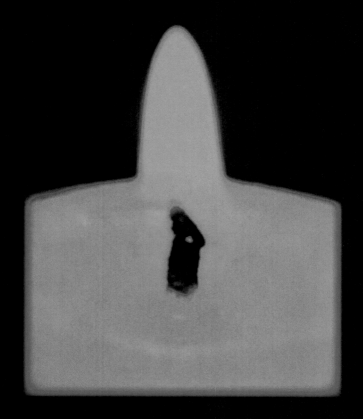

"Dear flame Rise in me. Grow Stronger.. and brighter each day..
each moment... Fill me up with love and joy.. Brighten my days..
Warm my heart.. Show me the way to be like you."

The illuminating flames of the candles, Ghee Lamps
carrying our prayers to the Heavens...

Lighting a candle is universal... and in use in most religions, temples,
sacred places, meditations, rituals, ceremonies, celebrations and more.

When you light a candle it refines the energy and makes things bright and
aglow.. it connects you to the Light and brings hope and joy within you..

The Flame loves to shine.

Lighting a candle sends a signal through our universe..
the light travels through time and space..

Shine your light.. It will be seen from wherever you
are.. Walk Aglow.. Wherever you'll be..

SHINE ON

The sun knows its power... Radiating endlessly... Ceaselessly shining.
Be the radiant Sun, endlessly shining the light from within.

'Come to me' Says the Flame. 'Come, sit close by me'.

'I have a story to tell you. Come, keep warm by the light'.

'The Heavens are watching us at all time...'

Personal quiet time - small Light Meditation

In your home, or other safe place, sit comfortably. (call upon your guardian angels, Jesus.. Archangels for protection).

Close your eyes, take a deep breath... inhale... And exhale... Gently repeat a few times.

Place your hands on your heart, continue breathing.. For a few more times. Inhale... exhale... relax your body.

As you continue to inhale and exhale,

Imagine you are inhaling — breathing in The light of GOD.

Breathe the light of GOD into your heart,..

Exhale any tension or worry that might have surfaced... Gently let it go.

Repeat for few more moments,

With each inhale you are calmer, more centered and relaxed.

Feel the light of GOD penetrating your heart... Feel the warmth and kind energy of GOD slowly expanding within you... you are being filled with love and feel the closeness to GOD.

Smile to your heart... Smile to the light of GOD. Feel the light keep expanding to your entire body... soak in this pure light. Feel the oneness you longed for.

Slowly, reach a little deeper as you are being lead to get in touch and connect with you inner life-Your essence life.. Which will lead you to your inner Flame..

It will happen when you'll be ready. Just flow... Relax, feel God's love within you. The light of God envelops you... your guardian angels surround you. You are Safe. Know within your heart that all is well. That God is taking care of you, and all your needs. God is omnipresent, omnipotent. With each breath you take, you breathe God's energy. You are divine, created in the image of GOD.

Take few moments to be with it, and remember you can always go back to that sacred place within you.

Slowly prepare yourself to end this meditation for now.

It's time to come back to the room where you started this small mediation, come back to your body. Become aware of your surroundings. The noise, the light, the sound, breathe in. Wiggle your toes. Wiggle your fingers. Come back. You are back now. Move your body. Open your eyes. You are back.

Thank your Angels. Your guides, the archangels, your masters for helping you meditate and reach within and for keeping you safe.

Thank GOD for his love and kindness. Thank Jesus and your masters and guides, and whomever you wish to express your gratitude, knowing one day, you'll connect and reach your Inner Flame..

You are calmer and refreshed. Walk in peace, knowing the Heavens are watching over you all the time. Walk in bliss. Shine your light.

Be thankful for your Inner Flame...

Tell God how much you love him... Feel your blessings all around.

If you take the time to meditate even for a little while each day to connect with your sacred inner life... One day, the Inner Door will open. You'll be filled with love, happiness and joy. You'll see the light within you, shining... You'll become aglow from within. You'll radiate the light of GOD more and more.. Wherever you'll be. No matter where you are, until one day you'll become one, in simile, Holy - In oneness with The Living Flame... one with GOD. Your life will transform. You'll be a radiant Light. You'll experience higher states of living and being.

Inner Journey...

Go within...

"Shine your Light no matter where you are"

Be the Light that you are... Never cease to shine. No matter what they say.

I choose to be a light.

I am living in the light.

I am a Light... created by the image of GOD.

I am a Light.

I better be glowing... than dimming my own light in fear that I might make someone become uncomfortable or aware of 'his or her' darkness, so they will get out of it and choose to live in the light.. (Some people will give you all sort of feedback... and say things from what lives in them.. and make you feel that you are 'too bright' or they might feel uncomfortable.. because suddenly you shine 'respectfully'...(naturally) into their life. Like a mirror, so they can change and make changes in their life to live a better Life. And heal and choose the light..) What I am trying to say is, don't dim you Light so others will feel comfortable in 'their darkness'. Choose to shine the Light. You Keep in the Light... They will have to make their choice what they want.

Just like the sun... the sun shines ceaselessly.. Never stop shining and glowing. Radiating and beaming light. Jesus never let anyone diminish Him or make Him forget His origin and His source — The Heavenly Father. Keep your connection to GOD... Alive and be Fully Connected. Keep the Flame of your connection with God and his kingdom alive... within you.

'The Sun shines upon All equally'.
Connect to the Sun of All Suns... Nourish your Inner Life...
It is the True meaning of Christ and the Christ
Consciousness - To be Holy, Illuminated from
Within... The I AM Presence within.
Radiating the great amount of God's Infinite
Light from Within... to Within...
You will become 'That Glowing Thing.. That BRIGHT
SHINING SUN IN GOD'S ENDLESS SKY'...

God...

My Lord,

How wonderful is your Creation.

Each dew drop,

Each rose,

Each wave,

Each ray of light travels freely,
meeting another with joy.

Each star...

Each leaf

Each flame,

Inspiring me... singing to me... so lovingly
joyous in me throughout eternity.

Thank you God for your endless flame within me...

The Sun is setting... Hope... Pray... Reach...
Imagine... a New Dawn... is coming...

The Light carries no weight.. Be like the Light.

Personal Message

The Flame speaks to you

The ocean sounds it's endless symphony..

Listen...

Birds fly by you... butterflies wings fluttering... gently fly closer to you.. Sometimes they land on your finger or your shoulder..

Life speaks gently. Yet, it is the most powerful gift of all.

The universe echoes your dreams, your songs;
your voice carries across all creation.

Keep gentle, full of love, the Flame asks. Yet strong and full of vigor like the fire.

Walk tall and ride courageously on the waves of life.

You are alive! In the midst of all there is!

Care to sing your song, Care to live your dreams, choose to be fulfilled...

Be that glorious flame that you are, shine on... a gift back to GOD.

Glory to GOD

Glory to the living flame

Glory to the gift of life

Hallowed be thy name

Holy Holy Holy...

You are in a Concert...

Listen how everything sings in Nature...
in the forest... in Creation.

Listen to the unheard Music.

Listen to the silence of the Flame.

Listen to the unheard rhythm of life.

Listen to the music within your heart..

Listen, to peace. Listen to love.
Listen to God's angels, listen to GOD.

Keep feeding your inner flame
with this marvelous creation.

There is so much to be inspired
by and be thankful to.

Pause a moment, through the rush of
your day. Stop and look at the beauty
of God's creation. Just for a moment,
become that quiet Flame... Silently, feel
the greatness all around you, in you...

Become aglow, centered in the river of
light that flows within you. Be like the
Flame that knows its source. Realize
your source... Remember it, Be it...

May your flame always glow.

May your light always shine.

May your tree forever grow.

May your river always flow.

May your song be sung.

May your story be heard.

May your heart always beat with joy.

May peace be your companion.

May harmony be your music.

May inspiration be your mover.

May bliss be your surroundings.

May your angels always guide and protect you.

May God's healing be your medicine..

May God bless you and always be with you.

May your life inspire others to live their life to the fullest.

Flames have no doubts they can shine..

Did you ever see a flame in doubt if it can glow today?

As you'll get in touch with your inner flame.. You'll become aware of the source of your Flame.. Just like all things in nature. Everything in nature knows they are in service and part of Creation.

Everything in Nature trusts GOD. Everything in Nature is being full and in wholeness with its gifts from GOD.

We were created in God's Image.
GOD gave us the Spirit of His Light
and His Glorious Flame... God
sealed us by His Holy Name.

Oh Glory to God in The Highest..

We are illuminated by
GOD'S grace and glory..

We are God's children..

We are the flames in God's
endless menorah... shining
in the spirit of life..

Angels gather by the light

Keeping warm by the Flame

Dancing, swirling all around..

'Living Fire'

Living Flame

Living Light

Living life all around..

The flame whispers LIVE! Dance! Gather by the light. Keep warm by the Flame. Keep closer and nearer to the source of your flame.

Angels are glowing from within... carrying the Light... Holding the Flame..

"There is wisdom in silence"...

the flame is silent.. if you make
your mark and sit by the flame..

One day the flame will speak.

The Flame will reveal a great wisdom..

You'll feel enhanced by the divine
connection to the glorious flame.

Solitude time.

Reflection in the Light.

There is time to be silent. There is time to speak.

Glowing and shining... is forever.

Shine from within... let go of all bitterness and hurt... what's the
point to hold onto other people's mistakes and wrong doing?

Life is precious. Choose to glow. Choose to be Happy. Let go of your unfortunate
aspects of your life. Move on. Take time to heal. Reach out to the Heavens,
to God, to heal. Tell a flame your story. Pray. Pray by a flame, it will carry
your prayer to GOD... God is omnipotent, omnipresent. God knows when
we are happy, God knows when we are hurting. God gave us free will, so
choose to be happy, glow... God loves to see us glowing... from far away...

Sit by the fire. Warm up... Listen to a good story teller... the night will become magical. The flame will illuminate the atmosphere. Listen to the Flame... Tell The Flame your story... The Flame is a good listener...

"Unseen Flames can be seen from inner vision.. "

Light up the flame in people's heart to love endlessly..

'*Never cease to Love... Never cease to Grow... Never cease to Glow...*'

"Be the igniter of your flame.. Be the Savior of your own Life..

Be the receiver of your miracles. Allow yourself to be happy, abundant, full of joy... watch the Flame. The Flame is being what it is as it meant to be... and doing what is meant to do... With so much love and confidence.. As it meant to do... You can do it to. You can be you. Discover the great you...

Be happy and free... Free your mind. Let the sacred flame in the middle of your crown, glow with much love... Feel the burning love within your being, shine... The Flame purifies your energy... The Flame reminds you of the love and the warmth within your heart... echoing with the flame.... Shinning together.... naturally...

Miracles are of the light... Blessings are of the light...

So, why one chooses to live in darkness?

God is happy when we are, God is happy when we are glowing.

God sees us all the time. Feel God's flame within your heart.

Become aware of GOD'S presence within you, making you Illuminated. Making you shine... By His Presence. In Him. With Him. You are a brilliant living light of GOD...

There is a flame to a flame, and a light to the light... Higher dimensions we can only see to a certain level. The physical level is limited on this earthly plan... Yet we can see though an inner vision to eternity. We can see through the spirit and the mind... we can see through the heart and our soul to higher dimensions all the way to eternity.

Can you imagine how the flame really looks in the spirit realm...?
Free your mind from limitation. Rise up and shine.. There is so much more
awaiting to be discovered. Choose to ride... freely.. Feel the light... Be the
light... Graceful being of GOD, you are a glowing flame in God's heart.

Looking into the flame

Wondering if it was here before...

The mind quiets down..

Slowing down, going inward, we go into a peaceful state of being...

Simply, peace is simple

Peaceful flame..

Dance, dance with me. Dance...

There is a longing in me to feel the warmth of the Flame.
To tell the Flame how much I love the Flame. Each time..

I kiss the Flame each time I light a candle by placing
my hands carefully above the flame.

I place my hands above the flame and gather the light and the warmth...
I bring it into me... and all over my being. I love the Flame... The Flame loves me.
We are enjoying each other's company... We are friends, we love each other
and are happy to see each other every and each time I light up a candle...
we smile and feel the warmth within our beings.. Being loved... recognizing each
other's life.. Happy to be... we shine... love makes us shine... so is the Flame...

Precious memories by the camp fire.. How wonderful was the warmth sitting by the fire. Watching the flames. singing. feeling delight... Precious memories of faces glowing by the fire.

God's precious love made the flame available for us to light a candle, to warm by the fire place or the camp fire, to watch the flame, to connect, to feel His warmth, to remember HIM, who created all things.

I Praise to GOD for the Flame...

Watching the Flame makes me wonder.. What does it tell? What shall I say to the Flame? I just sit silently, listening to its gentle dance... Then I closed my eyes... and I kept feeling the flame. Moving.. Dancing.. in me... I felt belonged as the Flame shared it's gift with me.. I love it and danced back in return.

Try to dance with a flame. Watch it move. Circling in one place. Keeping blue centered within. Feel the stillness of the flame from within radiating warmth and light. Stretching. Shrinking. Expanding. breathing. loving... joyfully. also there is no wind passing by. The flame is happy to be what it is... a flame.

What moves the flame? To what music does the flame dance? What does the dance mean? What does it say? Who dances by the Fire? Who sings by the flame? Who is it in the Flame..? ... I Wonder...

What moves the Flame?

Who is the mover of you?

What moves the sun?

Who is the mover of the universe?

I wonder...

Dear GOD,

Thank you for the Flame in my heart,
Thank you for the candle on my table.

Dear GOD,

Thank you for the dance of light within my soul. May the divine candle within my soul never be put down. May the flame within my soul ever glow, forever dance and shine..

Dear GOD, May your flame always illuminate within human hearts.

I Love You Lord. I thank you for your magnificent Creation. Thank you for the light within my being... and all around me. Thank you precious Lord for the Light of all Lights, Thank you for the Flame of All Flames and the Sun of All Suns..

Thank you GOD, for together with you, I can shine and be the Light that I am, where I am, wherever I be, as you made me be, illuminating by your glory through eternity.

GOD, you are the Immortal Bliss that makes all things shine..
You are GOD the Almighty. I salute your glorious being of Light...

God, You are the source of the candle...

The wax...

The wick...

And the flame...

You hold it together Lord. You hold it and light it up...

You are the Creator of my Life..

My body, my soul, my spirit and my light.

My flame, of who I am.. And all there is.

My precious Lord, envelope me with your being.

Fill me up with your presence.

Soak me in your glorious essence.

Dress me in your splendor. Make me glowing, vividly
radiating your love and light at service to you.

May your living flame surround me,

And be always present within me, illuminating in me forever.

Living flame of GOD,

I want to dance with you...

I want to sing with you, for you,

Forever, in-me. In me ay...

In me ay

In me ay

"I am a flame in GOD'S infinite Menorah..."

Oh Light... Om light... OM flame of all flames..

I AM THAT I AM

*Colors of the flame: gold and yellow, blue, green, red and orange…
different shades in different parts of the globe. Yet similar is the shape,
dance, size and purpose… always glowing upwards like a tree…*

*And we shall be… like a Living Candle that Never melts.. A Living Flame that
Never dies and A Living Tree that never withers.. always growing upwards…
and keeping bright, inspired by the cause and the source of our existence.. And
focused on the Heavens above … for the Heavens above are within us too…*

In Chanukah, Jewish people light up the menorah in remembrance of the miracles we had in the far past.

In all religions lighting a candle is a holy act in ceremonies, prayers, remembrance of the dead, celebrations and much more.

Light a candle each day. Pray. Connect with GOD. Expect miracles.

Celebrate the light. Celebrate your life. Celebrate the miracles yet to come.

Celebrate the living flames within your heart.

"Be the illuminated miracle within the center of your being".

Flame of wisdom, love and light, burning pure, burning bright.

I watch your beauty with great delight.. Oh glorious flame..
I dance with you... Gently my body moves... My inner life
awakens to your sight. I sit peacefully by your side...

Om Loving Light... I salute your glorious being shining light.

Watching the candle light. The healing flame... Looking at me... relaxing the rush of my day. With each candle I light up each day, I send a signal to the universe. As the light travels, my prayers are carried by the light to GOD...

My room becomes aglow by the Heavenly presences. Enveloping me with warmth and feeling delight.. I express my gratitude for the Heavens beauty right here. Each day, each night, creating Heaven on Earth wherever I am. My Precious Lord loves me so much... Oh, I wish to remain aglow... And shining so bright in return for my life..

I sing to the flame. I sing to GOD, how marvelous your creation is. Each time, each flame anew like each dew... endlessly travels back to you, wherever you are. In me, in you.. My GOD I love you.

My lord just like the Flame... Each time I light up a candle, something in me lights up too.. Sometimes, if I have a long or a hard day... or even when if for a moment or two, if I fell into feelings of doubts.. When I light a candle... I calm down, and feel Hope.. It brings me back.. To you!

I feel your presence. For YOU ARE THE LIGHT... the little flame in my room is just a tiny little spark of your glorious infinite light. I feel peace, knowing you are in the Flame.. The Flame is in you... in me.

Thank you Heavenly Father... For the Illuminating Flames..

Thank you GOD for The LIGHT.

*My dear Heavenly Father, Thank you for the matches you
provide for me that I can light up my candles each day...*

*Each day I light a candle in memory of my greatest teachers and honoring
my ancestors and guides, my beings of light and people that I love.*

Remembering is a holy act of caring, respecting and keeping their light alive...

Flames are holy... at service to life.

I meet people that inspired me. Their life empowered me with their glowing light; they are always alive in me... I love their light..

Light goes to light..

I met people that forgot their light.. They were down.. Living in dark shady places within them.. I reached out to light their life... some raised up and became more and more light.

There were those.. Who were so deep in the dark.. That they tried to bring me down and hurt me. They didn't like that I was glowing and bright. I had to shield myself and learned to ask my guides if it was meant to be? If I supposed to bring to them the light.. My Angels said — "Never stop shining. Never stop glowing.. No matter where you are, yet, use discernment. Fear Not. Be careful and always be on guard. Sometimes, just "See it.. Know it.. (That dark shady thing).. But don't deal..." Don't allow it any near... (It won't stand the light anyway..) Be the light that you are.. Wherever you are... The light protects you. We, the angels of GOD, surround you. We are always with you. Fear not, for in the light you are in oneness with GOD and no dark thing can exist in the light".

I want to be where it is natural for me to be... where I feel myself.. Where I feel belong.. With the light.. In The LIGHT..

Belonging, longing for the light.. I sit by a Flame where I feel belonged...

Singing makes the flame dance....

Music, makes the Flame.. sing...

The Flame is musical..

Sacred dance of the Flame, dancing within my soul....

My heart sings.. I rejoice by the light of the Flame..

How wonderful is the sight of the Flame...

Graceful dance of light beings.. Circling the Flame, dancing.. Among the stars..

The Flame is a good Listener...

The Flame is a good audience..

The Flame is a great Performer...

I am inspired by a Flame.

The Flame smiles to me.

'Laughing flames', joyfully being alive...

The Flame is happy to be what it is.

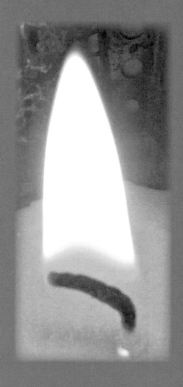

Inspired by the Flame.. I lay down to sleep.. I watch the calming light. Peace fills up my room. I wonder, what will I dream of this night? Where will I go? The Flame knows my inner life. It can feel me just like the trees and the flowers.. Just like all creatures, they can see my light. They feel and see..

I love to shine. I love to be as I am meant to be - a glowing light. I love... I light...' I flame'... I can. God made me this way. I am happy to be me and shine my own light... Light goes to Light. The Light shines to all like the Sun which shines upon all Living equally.

I'll be the sun.

I'll be the caressing wind.

I'll be the ocean waves... Reaching ashore..

I'll be the Flame. Glowing, igniting other lives to shine on...

Radiating the greatness that I AM with.

I'll be the song that God sings within my soul...

Emanating from the Living Fire...' In Me Ay'...

I AM that I AM Wherever I go.

Wherever I be.

GOD is IN ME.. I AM In GOD

As I am..

As God Would have me Be. As I AM 'little me' as - Created by Him, in His Image.

As Him. In Him.. Eternally.. Om Light.. Illuminated Way.. In Me Ay

A warm smile is like a flame.. Full of love.. Warming your heart..

Making Your eyes glow like the stars..

Keep Your Flame ALIVE...

Remember the source of your Flame.

Be that light..

And the Lord said, 'To Eternity!!!'

"… And your name shall be like the sun, shining upon all…

Your song will be like the light, glowing in people's heart..

And your life will touch all life…

For I AM in you. You are IN ME..

I make you known like the stars in the endless sky… Forever glowing..

Creation is echoing your song… Wherever you'll go. Wherever you be..

My dear child of light. you have my blessings… You have
my name upon your being… I AM present in you.. With you
and all around you, no matter where you are…

You sing my song to all living.. With so much love… And I sing with you…

You sing my song… you light my candles… you bring light wherever you go..

For I love you dearly my dear child.

You are a glowing Flame within my Heart…" Said the LORD.

"Leave a trail of Light behind you for others to find their way.."/Rev. Kemi Nahal

Photo Credits

Photos by Rev. Kemi Nahal: Pages 2, 8, 19, 24, 25, 27, 28, 29, 30, 31, 32, 33, 34, 35, 40, 42, 46, 49, 50, 51, 53, 60, 65, 67, 73, 78, 81, 89, 90

Photos by Oriya Nahal – Bartow: Pages 29, 49

Photos by Vladimir Kush: Cover, Page 6

Photos by Erica Rappaport: Pages 1, 3, 4, 9, 10, 11, 13, 14, 16, 17, 18, 20, 21, 22, 23, 26, 36, 37, 38, 39, 41, 43, 44, 45, 52, 54, 55, 56, 57, 58, 59, 61, 62, 63, 64, 66, 68, 69, 70, 71, 72, 74, 75, 76, 77, 79, 80, 82, 84, 85, 87, 88